Outside and Inside WOOLLY MAMMOTHS

Sandra Markle

 WALKER & COMPANY
New York

This is the preserved body of a baby woolly mammoth (MA-meth), nicknamed Dima. Its body lay frozen and buried in the earth for thousands of years—so long that its muscles shriveled and dried. It also lost most of the long, shaggy coat of hair that covered its body. You can clearly see woolly mammoths were a kind of elephant, but they're extinct, meaning none are left alive.

So what happened to woolly mammoths? In this book, you'll find out what science and technology have helped scientists discover about woolly mammoths, why scientists think they may have become extinct, and why some researchers think woolly mammoths could one day roam the Earth again.

The word *mammoth* has come to mean something that's huge, but woolly mammoths weren't any taller or heavier than living elephants. From frozen remains and skeletons, scientists have determined that males were bigger than females, and the largest male woolly mammoths were about 9 to 11 feet (2.7 to 3.4 meters) tall at the shoulder. Alive, they probably weighed an estimated 5 to 6 tons (4,536 to 5,443 kilograms). That makes them about the size of this big male African elephant. Male Asian elephants are a little shorter and lighter. A woolly mammoth's shape was a little different from that of living elephants, though. Woolly mammoths had a slightly more sloping back.

Look at this preserved woolly mammoth head. See how little its ear is! It is only about 12 inches (30.5 centimeters) long. The largest preserved mammoth ear ever found is only a little bigger—about 15 inches (38 centimeters) long.

How does this compare to elephants' ears? Asian elephants, like this one, have much smaller ears than do African elephants (like the one on page 5). African elephants' ears are nearly 6 feet (1.8 meters) long. Asian elephants' ears are about 2.5 feet (0.76 meter) long. So a woolly mammoth's ears were much smaller than those of living elephants. That was probably an adaptation to living where it was frequently cold and any part that stuck out from their shaggy coat would have become chilled.

Now, look closely at this African elephant's ear and you'll see there is a network of blood vessels sandwiched between layers of skin. By holding its ears away from its body, an African or Asian elephant lets air cool the blood flowing through its ear. Then that cooler blood moves through the rest of its big body to help cool it off.

Woolly mammoth ears had this same structure. If you've ever bundled up for cold weather and then been active, you know you can overheat even though the air temperature is cold. That likely happened to woolly mammoths because they had a triple layer of hair plus a thick insulating layer of fat under their skin to trap their body heat. So, like living elephants, woolly mammoths probably used their ears to cool off when they were hot.

Could having a body designed to hold on to heat and with a very small cooling system have caused problems for woolly mammoths once the climate started to warm up? How else might a climate change have affected woolly mammoths?

Scientists have studied the area where woolly mammoth bones and preserved remains have been found, the area highlighted in gold on the map. But when mammoths lived in that area—what scientists named the mammoth steppe—it was colder and drier during the winter. While warmer seasons were likely cool and dry, the ground thawed deep enough to support a variety of plant life, especially grasses. Researchers believe summertime may have looked a lot like this summertime view of Wrangel Island. Lying north of the Arctic Circle, Wrangel Island is believed to have changed very little since the Pleistocene (PLYS-tuh-seen)—from about 1.8 million years ago to about 10,000 years ago—when the world was colder than it is now and there were many periods now known as ice ages. Woolly mammoths are believed to have lived during the Pleistocene.

Today, though, no place on Earth—not even Wrangel Island—has exactly the same mix of plants that made up the menu for these giant herbivores (ER-beh-vors), or plant eaters.

mammoth
steppe

Scientists learned that the digestive system of a living elephant fully breaks down less than half of the plant material it swallows. They guessed the same was true for woolly mammoths.

Check out this material from the Yukagir mammoth's intestine. Researcher Bas Van Geel used chemicals and fine-meshed sieves to separate out the undigested bits of plant matter and examined them under a microscope. This way, he was able to identify the plant material in the mammoth's last meal. This included willow-tree buds and leaves; buttercups; bits of moss; and pollen grains, the reproductive cells from flowering plants. But the majority of the material was grass. Living elephants eat a varied diet, but Bas Van Geel and other scientists have discovered that woolly mammoths ate lots of grass. When researchers studied the intestines of another frozen mammoth, the Shandrin mammoth, they discovered most of the nearly 600 pounds (272 kilograms) of partly digested food they contained were grass.

Scientists also learned that woolly mammoths had features that made them especially suited to the food they ate. For one thing, the tip of a woolly mammoth's trunk had a unique shape. Look closely at these two African elephants and you'll see their trunks end in two equally long tips. Look back on page 7 to see that an Asian elephant's trunk has just one tip. Then take another look at the tip of Dima's twisted trunk on page 2. Woolly mammoth trunks had one long and one short tip. That gave woolly mammoths a sort of thumb-and-finger arrangement.

To see the difference in how these trunk tips function, try to pick up something like a coin with just your index finger. Next, try again using your index and middle fingers. Finally, use your thumb and index finger. The woolly mammoth's trunk must have been especially suited to grabbing and pulling up the extremely short mammoth steppe grasses. It also would have been perfectly suited to plucking the small wildflowers and willow buds Bas Van Geel discovered in the Yukagir mammoth's intestine.

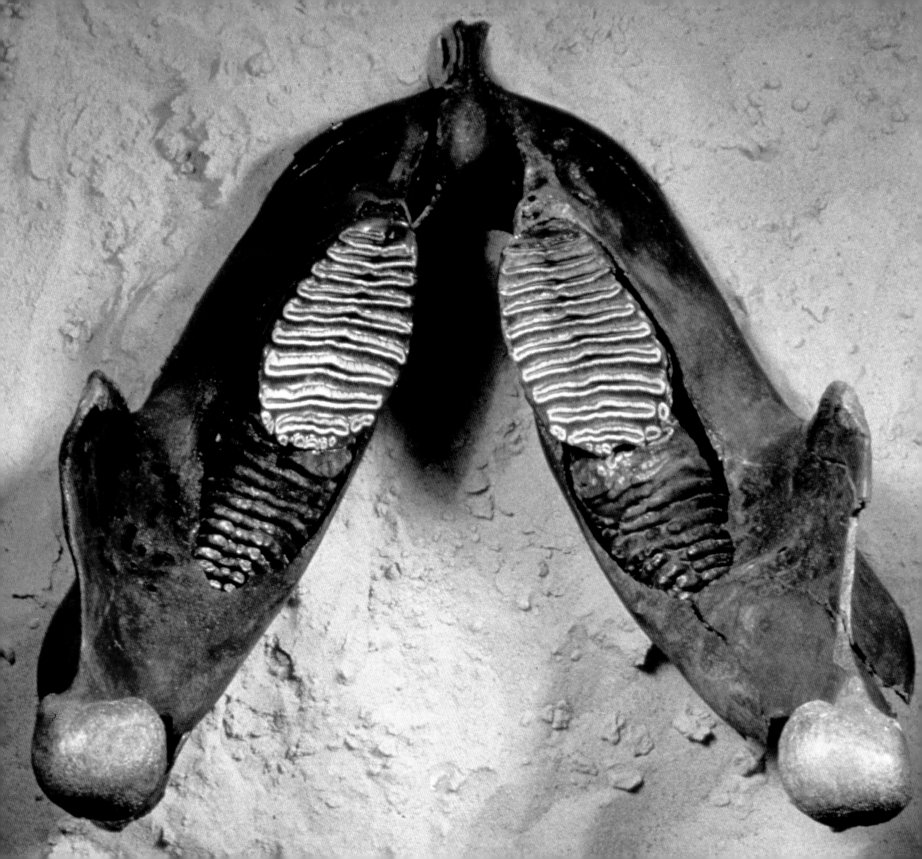

From examining preserved mammoth jawbones, like this lower jawbone, scientists discovered that a woolly mammoth's jaw structure was very similar to that of living elephants. Like African and Asian elephants, woolly mammoths chewed with just four molars at a time—one on each side of their left and right, upper and lower jaws. As each tooth became worn, it moved forward in the jaw. For a while, the mammoth chewed on the back part of the old molar and the front part of the new, emerging molar. Eventually, the mammoth spat out the worn-down old tooth, and the new one replaced it. Here you can see two of the molars that were in use and the new ones that were developing behind them.

Researchers have also learned that, like living elephants, woolly mammoths usually had six sets of molars during their lifetime. Compare the molars from a baby, young adult, and mature adult woolly mammoth. The sixth and final molars were the biggest—each about a foot long (30 centimeters) and weighing about 5 pounds (2.3 kilograms). Like the molars of living elephants, woolly mammoth molars were made up of enamel plates. But mammoth molars had a lot more of those plates. Enamel is a super-hard material that made mammoth molars perfect for grinding up all the grass they ate. Grass contains bits of sandlike silica, which make it much rougher than leaves of other plants.

Could having a body suited to eating certain kinds of plants and then having that food supply change have caused woolly mammoths to become extinct?

young adult

baby

mature adult

Here you can see yet another part of woolly mammoths that researchers have studied—their tusks. Tusks are actually giant incisors, or front teeth. Like living elephants' tusks, these are made of ivory. But woolly mammoth tusks grew longer and more twisted than any living elephant's tusks. They were also heavier. The longest recorded woolly mammoth tusk was 16 feet (4.9 meters) long and weighed 208 pounds (94.4 kilograms).

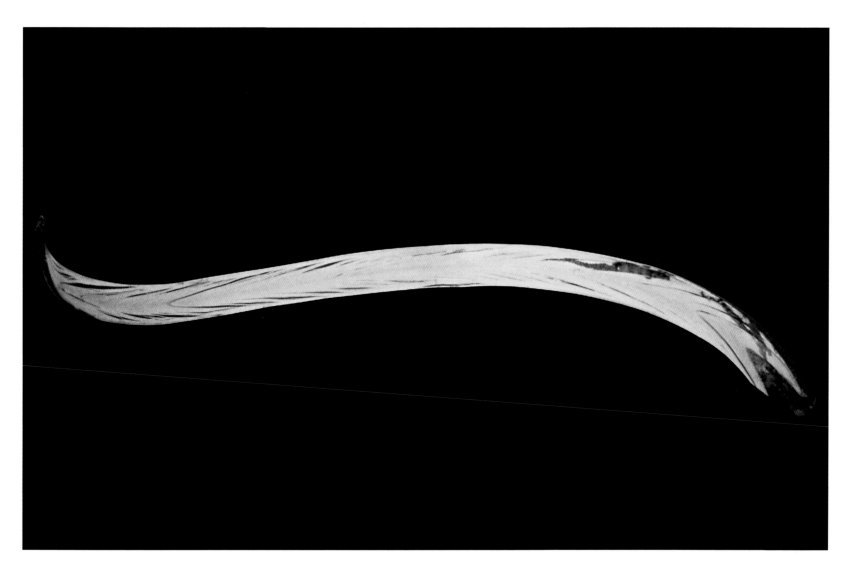

In this sliced-open tusk, you can see what researcher Dan Fisher discovered—its stacked-cone structure. Like those of living elephants, the tusks of woolly mammoths grew from the base out by adding new tooth material, or dentin (DEN-ten), to form a cone shape. Then, like building a tower of ice cream cones by adding onto the bottom of the stack, additional cones were formed. And the tusk grew longer.

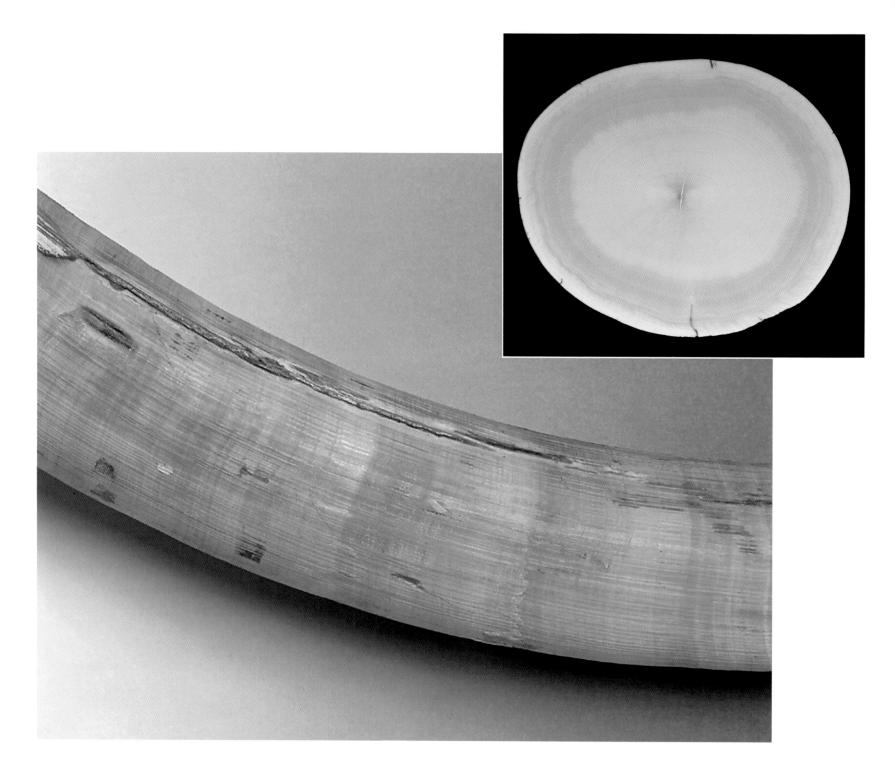

Dan Fisher wanted to see if all of that dentin being deposited throughout a woolly mammoth's life might reveal something about its personal history. So he cut very thin disks from a number of different woolly mammoth tusks and examined these under a microscope. He learned that the tusks grew by adding a ring of new dentin every day. And these rings formed bands of weekly sets of growth rings. Fisher discovered some bands were wider than others. He believed this was caused by times when food was plentiful and times when it was scarce.

Could a diminishing food supply have caused woolly mammoths to become extinct?

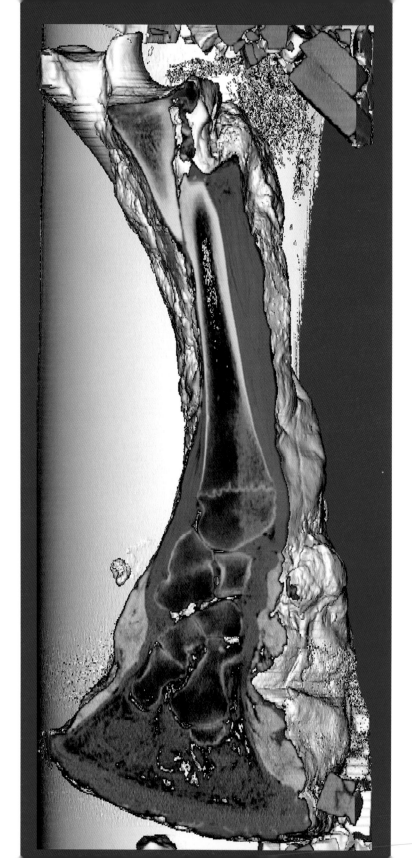

Next, look inside the Yukagir mammoth's left front leg. Naoki Suzuki made this image of the inside of the mammoth's leg using a special kind of X-ray machine called a spiral computed tomography (toh-MA-gre-fee) scanner, also called a spiral CT scanner. A CT scanner is made up of an X-ray-generating tube that continuously orbits the specimen, taking many images, which are then recorded digitally by a computer. The computer is programmed to display images that show only materials of specific densities. This is the way that Naoki Suzuki created a three-dimensional image of the internal structure of the Yukagir mammoth's leg bones and the attached muscles that moved them. And he did it without cutting into the leg or damaging it.

Researchers already knew from assembled skeletons that, like living elephants, mammoths walked on their tiptoes. Beneath the toes is a pad of fatty and fibrous tissue that's especially thick at the back—like a shoe with a wedge-shaped heel. By studying the CT scan, Naoki Suzuki learned something new. The Yukagir mammoth had about a 13 percent larger sole than that of living elephants. This probably acted like a snowshoe to spread out the mammoth's weight and keep it from sinking as deeply into snow or mud as it might have otherwise.

Then Naoki Suzuki used the computerized three-dimensional images of the mammoth's leg to do something that had never been done before. He programmed the computer to make the leg muscles move the leg bones. That way he was able to see the way the mammoth's leg would have moved when it was alive. And he learned woolly mammoths walked in a way that was very similar to how living elephants walk.

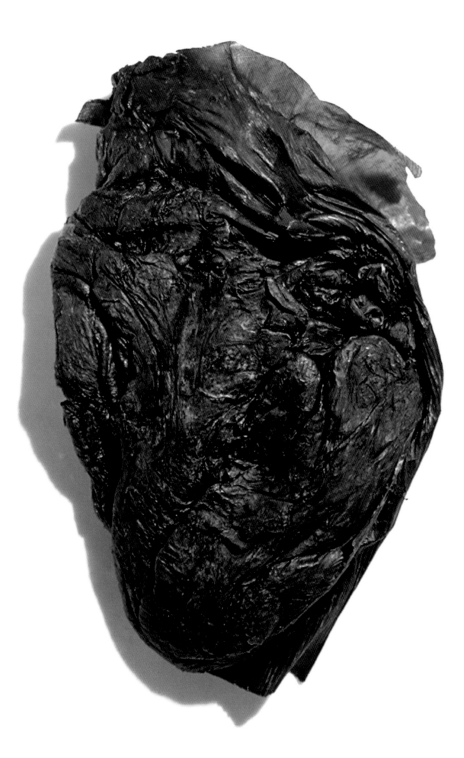

Check this out! It's the baby woolly mammoth Dima's heart. Naoki Suzuki studied it too. He discovered that it was larger than the heart of a similarly sized baby African or Asian elephant. He believed having a supersized heart was another adaptation to living in a cold environment. A bigger heart would pump more warm blood with each beat, helping to keep the mammoth's body warm.

Could that have been another physical feature that caused problems for woolly mammoths as the climate warmed up?

Naoki Suzuki decided to study the internal structure of Dima's heart. So he used the CT scanner to generate a three-dimensional view of the interior. This showed that, even though it was larger, the structure of the woolly mammoth's heart was identical to that of living elephants, including a unique feature. Like you, elephants have a four-chambered heart made up of two upper and two lower chambers. However, in your heart, the lower chambers, called ventricles, are joined together, forming one point. In elephants and woolly mammoths, the two ventricles are separate, so the bottom of the heart has two points.

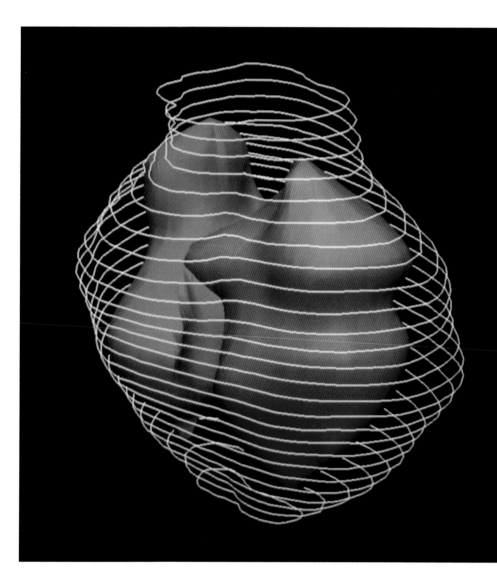

Here's a surprise researcher Jeheskel Shoshani found by accident: woolly mammoth blood. He was studying Dima's muscle tissue using a scanning electron microscope, an instrument able to magnify from 10,000 to 1,000,000 times, depending upon its quality level. Suddenly, he saw red blood cells. His first thought was that whoever had prepared the slide had cut his or her finger and gotten blood on the slide. Then he saw that the blood cells were inside a capillary, a small blood vessel, in the muscle tissue. So Jeheskel Shoshani knew the blood cells belonged to Dima. He was surprised because usually blood cells break down after so much time. He was excited to be able to compare them to the blood cells of living elephants. He discovered they were identical.

blood cell

Now, look at these scanning electron microscope views of the Jarkov mammoth's hairs. These highlight the biggest difference of all between woolly mammoths and living elephants. While living elephants have only a sparse coat, woolly mammoths had a coat made up of three kinds of hair. Guard hairs, which formed a protective, water-repellent coat, ranged from a few inches (a few centimeters) long on the ears and trunk to 3 feet (0.9 meter) long on the body. The body hairs, which acted like a warm sweater, were thinner than the guard hairs and were only up to a foot (0.3 meter) long. The woolly undercoat hairs, which acted like thermal underwear, were much shorter—from just 1 to 3 inches (2.5 to 8 centimeters) long. Further analysis of the hairs revealed something exciting—DNA, the chemical code of all cells.

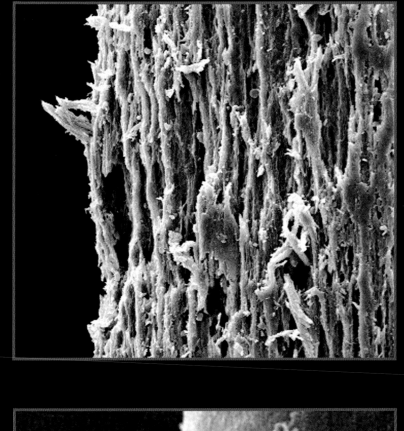

guard hair

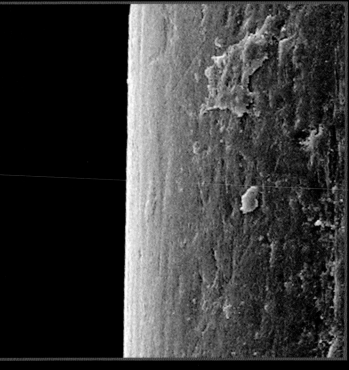

body hair

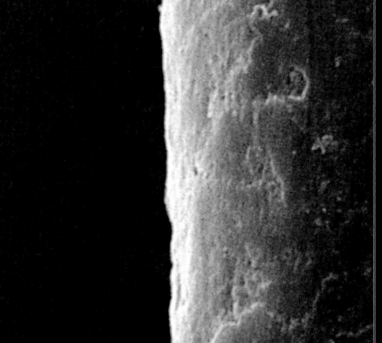

undercoat hair

33

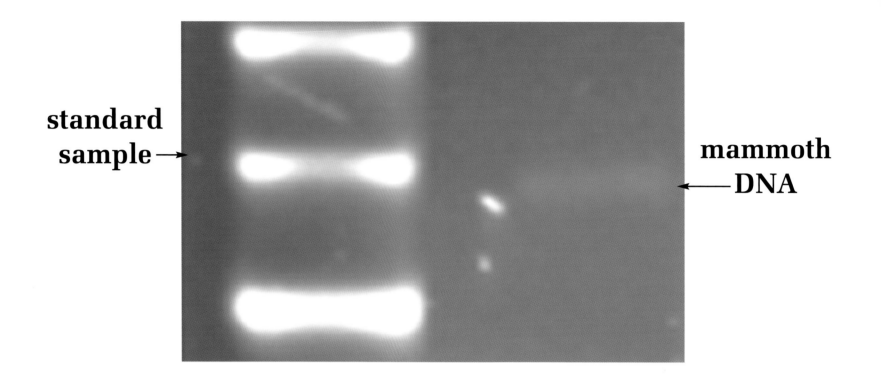

standard sample →

mammoth ← DNA

Could the fact that woolly mammoths were genetically different from living elephants be the reason they are extinct?

The pale white line is a sample of ancient woolly mammoth DNA prepared by Alex Greenwood. It's next to a standard sample scientists use for comparison. Although the mammoth DNA sample doesn't look like much, seeing it was a first for scientists studying woolly mammoths, and they were excited to have an opportunity to analyze it. When they compared woolly mammoth DNA to the DNA of living elephants, they got a surprise. The genetic code was very similar. In fact, it was so similar some scientists are eager to try an experiment.

They want to try placing woolly mammoth DNA in a living elephant's egg cell. That would produce a clone, a baby elephant that has woolly mammoth traits. If it is possible to clone a woolly mammoth, then scientists will be able to study the living animal and, hopefully, understand woolly mammoths much better. Maybe they'll finally discover a difference that could have led to their extinction. So far, though, a baby woolly mammoth has not been cloned.

Even with all that's been discovered about woolly mammoths, why these animals became extinct remains a mystery. Scientists have three main theories. Some think early man hunted them to extinction. Others think a disease wiped them out, although no one has yet been able to find evidence of any particular disease organisms in preserved mammoths.

Still others think that when the weather changed, so did the plant life—to the extent that mammoths became limited to pockets of suitable plants. Eventually, the mammoth population shrank until the few survivors died or were hunted and killed.

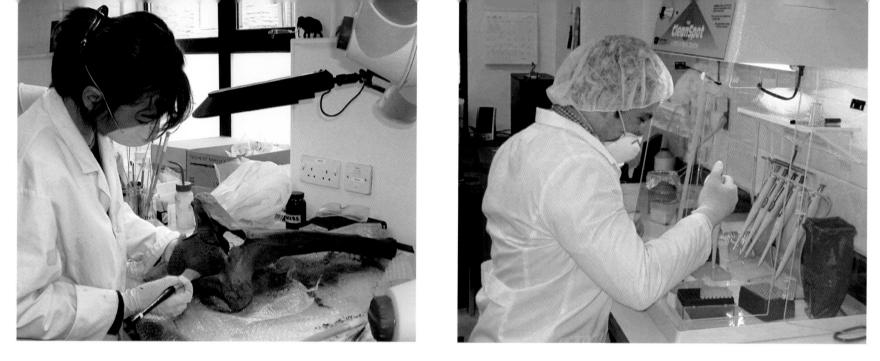

Who knows? One day, you could be the one to collect clues about woolly mammoths that finally prove why they became extinct, like this scientist studying these giants' bones or the one investigating mammoth DNA. Or you might be the one to tackle the challenge of whether woolly mammoths could be cloned and survive. Then a whole new generation of woolly mammoths might roam the Earth.

Glossary/Index

BONE   *bone*   One of the hard parts that forms the body's supporting frame or skeleton. **10, 17, 25, 26**

CT SCAN   *see-TEE skan*   An image produced through computer processing of X-ray images. **26**

DNA   *de-en-A*   The abbreviation for the long chemical name (deoxyribonucleic acid) of the special part of every cell that stores all of the information needed for the cell to function. Also controls inherited traits. **32, 34, 35**

HAIR   *hare*   The threadlike outgrowths of skin cells in some kinds of animals. **3, 9, 32, 33**

HEART   *hart*   A muscular body part that contracts in a repeated, rhythmic pattern to pump blood through the body's network of blood vessels. **28, 29**

INTESTINE   *in-TES-tun*   The body part where special juices finish breaking down food into nutrients. **13, 15**

MAMMOTH STEPPE   *MA-meth step*   The unique environment during the ice ages that was the mammoths' habitat. **10, 11, 15**

PLEISTOCENE   *PLYS-tuh-seen*   The geologic period during the Earth's past that began about 1.8 million years ago and ended about 10,000 years ago. **10**

TEETH   *teeth*   The hard, bony structures in the jaws used for grinding up food. **20**

TRUNK   *trunk*   The muscular, elongated body part in mammoths and living elephants formed by the fusion of the upper lip and nose. **15, 32**

TUSK   *tusk*   A greatly enlarged and elongated tooth that projects from the mouth. **20, 21, 23, 39**

More Woolly Facts

Woolly mammoths (*Mammuthus primigenius*) weren't the only kind of mammoths. There were others, including the Columbian mammoth (*Mammuthus columbi*). Adult Columbian mammoths were less hairy but usually taller and heavier than woolly mammoths—about 14 feet (4 meters) at the shoulder and weighing as much as 10 tons (9,072 kilograms). They ranged much farther south than woolly mammoths did, roaming across the midwestern United States into Mexico and even Central America.

Mammoths were named after the ancient Russian word for *earth*. Because their remains were found in the earth, people once believed mammoths had lived in burrows underground.

Remains of dwarf-sized woolly mammoths have been found on Wrangel Island. They were just 70 inches (178 centimeters) tall at the shoulder. Radiocarbon dating shows these mammoths were alive until between 7,000 and 3,700 years ago. So they may have been among the last to become extinct and could have been alive while the ancient Egyptians were building the pyramids.

For More Information

To find out more about woolly mammoths and the time they lived, check out the following resources.

BOOKS

Agenbroad, Larry, and Lisa W. Nelson. *Mammoths: Ice-Age Giants*. Minneapolis, MN: Lerner, 2002. An overview of what scientists have discovered from the remains of woolly mammoths.

Chorlton, Windsor. *Mammoths*. New York: Scholastic Reference, 2003. Discover the story of the Jarkov mammoth.

Miller, Debbie. *A Woolly Mammoth Journey*. Boston: Little, Brown, 2001. Enjoy a fictionalized story about a woolly mammoth family that provides an interesting view of what this extinct animal's life was like.

WEB SITES

Ice Age Mammals
www.zoomdinosaurs.com/subjects/mammals/Iceagemammals.shtml   Discover some of the fascinating animals that lived alongside woolly mammoths.

Mammoth Fun
http://school.discovery.com/schooladventures/woollymammoth/   The Discovery School's interactive activities let you investigate a woolly mammoth's ancestors and migration. Links provide a guide to other worthwhile Web explorations.

Virtually in the Ice Age
http://www.creswell-crags.org.uk/virtuallytheiceage/   Step back in time to tour Creswell Crags, a limestone gorge in England, during the ice ages. Get to know the animals and the people living there during that ancient time.

With special appreciation to the editors whom, through my years of working on this series, I've come to value as friends: Sharon Steinhoff, Marcia Marshall, and Emily Easton.

First published in the United States of America in 2007 by
Walker Publishing Company, Inc.
Distributed to the trade by Holtzbrinck Publishers

For information about permission to reproduce selections from this book, write to Permissions, Walker & Company, 104 Fifth Avenue, New York, New York 10011

All papers used by Walker & Company are natural, recyclable products made from wood grown in well-managed forests. The manufacturing processes conform to the environmental regulations of the country of origin.

Library of Congress Cataloging-in-Publication Data
Markle, Sandra.
Outside and inside woolly mammoths / by Sandra Markle.
p.   cm.
ISBN-13: 978-0-8027-9589-2 • ISBN-10: 0-8027-9589-7 (hardcover)
ISBN-13: 978-0-8027-9590-8 • ISBN-10: 0-8027-9590-0 (reinforced)
1. Woolly mammoth—Juvenile literature. I. Title.
QE882.P8M37 2007   569'.67—dc22   2006027621

Book design by Nicole Gastonguay

Visit Walker & Company's Web site at www.walkeryoungreaders.com

Printed in China
10 9 8 7 6 5 4 3 2 1

Acknowledgments: The author would like to thank the following people for sharing their expertise and enthusiasm: Dr. Larry Agenbroad, Northern Arizona University and the Mammoth Site; William Boismier, Norfolk Quarry Mammoth Project; Dr. James Burns, the Provincial Museum of Alberta; Dr. Daniel Fisher, University of Michigan; Dr. Adrian Lister, University College, London; Dr. Paul Martin, University of Arizona; Dr. James Mead, Northern Arizona University; Mr. Dick Mol, Natural History Museum, Rotterdam; Dr. Hendrik Poinar, McMaster University, Ontario; Dr. Jeheskel Shoshani, University of Asmara; Dr. Naoki Suzuki, Jikei University School of Medicine, Tokyo; Dr. Alexi Tikhonov, Scientific Secretary, Mammoth Committee, Russian Academy of Sciences, Saint Petersburg; Dr. Bas van Geel, University of Amsterdam; and the Zoological Institute of Russian Academy of Sciences. Finally, a special thanks to Skip Jeffery, who shared the effort and joy of creating this book.

Note to Parents and Teachers: The books in the Outside and Inside series enable young readers to discover how scientists, often working as a team, use different methods or procedures to investigate and sometimes develop new technologies or procedures to enable them to learn even more.

Photo Credits

Cover:	Jonathan Blair/Corbis	
Page 1:	John Cancalosi/Nature Picture Library	
Page 2:	Alexei Tikhanov and Institute Zoologic	
Page 5:	Joe McDonald	
Page 6:	Naoki Suzuki	
Page 7:	Konrad Wothe/Minden	
Page 8:	Joe McDonald	
Page 11:	Roger Tidman/Corbis; inset Sandra Markle	
Page 12:	Martin Harvey/Corbis	
Page 13:	Bas van Geel & Jan van Arkel, IBED,	

Universiteit van Amsterdam
Page 14: Nigel J. Dennis-Gallo Images/Corbis
Page 16: Adrian Lister
Page 19: Mike Newton/Marshall Editions
Page 20: Francis Latreille/Novi Productions
          REUTERS/Corbis
Page 21: Dan Fisher
Page 22: Mike Newton/Marshall Editions; inset
          Dan Fisher
Page 24: Naoki Suzuki

Page 27: Martin Harvey-Gallo Images/Corbis
Page 28: Naoki Suzuki
Page 29: Naoki Suzuki
Page 31: Marion Barnhart-Jeheskel Shoshani
Page 33: Hair supplied by Larry Agenbroad (SEM by
          Simon Pollard)
Page 34: Alex Greenwood
Page 35: Martin Harvey-Gallo Images/Corbis
Page 37: Alex Greenwood; Sonia O'Connor

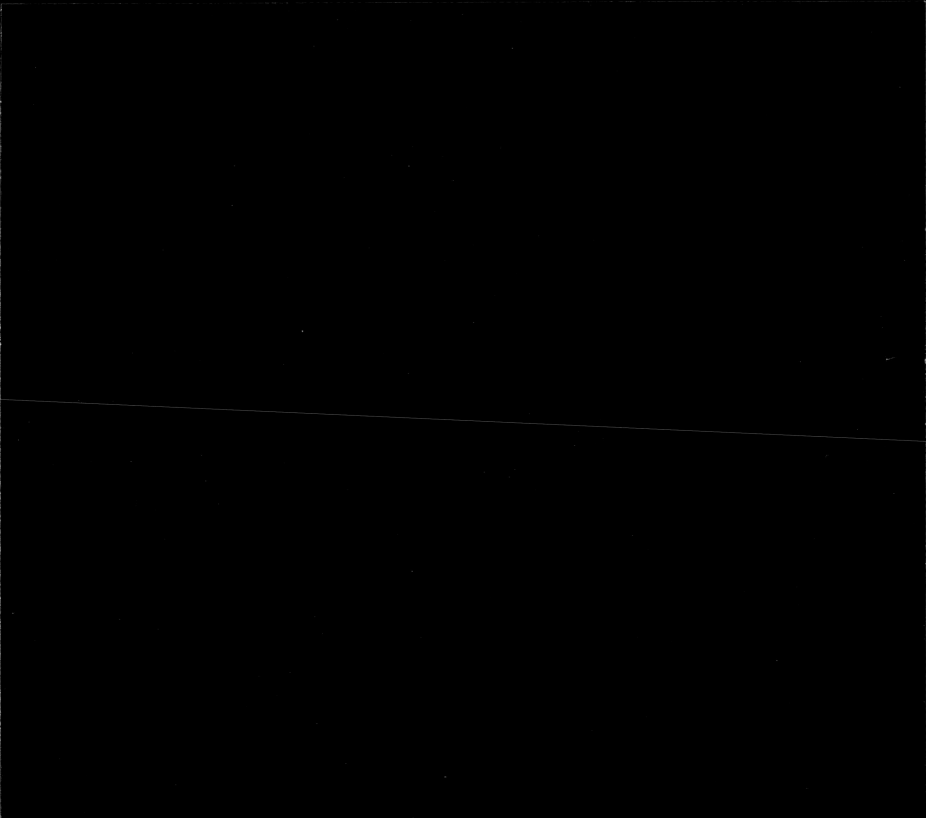